• Contents •

To Mark, my favorite reluctant reader.

Fine Feathered
Four Eyes
Starring...

And introducing...

Chapter 1
Oops

"It's handball time!" Nate shouted to his friend Benny B. Benjamin. "Let's play!"

Benny stayed on the bench, not even lifting his head. "No handball for me today. I'm busy reading about Albert Einstein's theory of relativity."

Nate sighed. "It's recess. Time to have fun."

Benny turned the pages of a thick book and muttered, "Einstein sure wrote some interesting stuff."

"I wish you weren't so smart," Nate told Benny.

Then Nate turned to Jason Johnson, who was sitting next to Benny and staring at the math textbook. "Jason, will you play handball with me?" he asked.

"I'd love to," Jason said.

"Great!" Nate exclaimed.

"But I can't," Jason said. "I have to study for the math test Mrs. Crabpit is giving us tomorrow. My parents said that if I don't pass the test, they'll cancel my birthday party. And it's going to be the best party ever. I'm going to have a huge cake with extra frosting, a dragon piñata filled with a ton of candy and real money, make-your-own sundaes with seven kinds of ice cream and thirty-eight toppings, and six different video games going at all times with six pro gamers helping us."

"Keep studying," Nate said. "I don't want to miss out on that party."

Nate felt so desperate, he asked his twin sister, Lisa, if she'd play handball with him.

But Lisa was busy talking to her best friend, Ashley Chang. Actually, Ashley was talking to Lisa. And talking. And talking. And talking.

So Nate picked up the rubber ball and bounced it to the handball court by himself.

"Nate! Be careful with that ball!" Lisa shouted. "It's bouncing really close to where we're sitting."

What a worrywart, Nate thought. He knew how to control the ball. He just wished he could control his friends and make them play handball with him. He bounced the ball hard against the handball court.

"Be careful!" Lisa yelled.

Nate thought about Jason's birthday party. He pictured the sundae he'd make. It would include all seven kinds of ice cream and every topping there was. Except nuts, because he didn't like nuts.

He bounced the ball again.

"Be careful!" Lisa yelled louder.

His sundae wouldn't have celery on it either.

Wait a minute. Celery wasn't a sundae topping.

Good. He hated celery.

He bounced the ball again.

4

"Be careful!" Lisa yelled even louder.

"Yah!" Jason shouted.

Oops. Somehow, the handball had landed right next to Jason.

At least it didn't hit him, Nate thought.

"The handball hit me!" Jason yelled.

Oops. "Well, at least nothing got broken," Nate said to himself.

"The ball broke my glasses!" Jason shrieked.

Oops. *Well, Jason could probably get by without his glasses,* Nate thought.

"I'm practically blind without my glasses!" Jason cried.

Oops. "Well, not being able to see anything for a few days won't be that bad," Nate said to himself.

"Now I'll fail the math test tomorrow for sure," Jason wailed. "And my parents will cancel my birthday party, and I won't get a huge cake with extra frosting, a dragon piñata filled with a ton of candy and real money, make-your-own sundaes with seven kinds of ice cream and thirty-eight toppings, and six different video games going at all times with six pro gamers helping us."

"I'm really sorry," Nate said. He felt awful, so awful he didn't think it was possible to feel any worse.

"You destroyed the party of the century, Nate," Michael Perez said.

"I've been looking forward to that party for weeks," Dan the Dawdler said.

"Yeah, what *he* said," Grant Sinker said.

"Ditto," Jason Johnson said.

"Exactly," Michael Perez said.

Okay, it had been possible to feel worse. *Now* Nate believed he couldn't feel any worse.

"I warned you to be careful with that handball," Lisa said. "Told you so, told you so, told you so."

And now Nate felt even worse.

Chapter 2

Plop the Farting Dog

"I told you to be careful with the ball," Lisa told Nate as they rode the school bus home. "But you didn't listen to me. Now Jason's glasses are ruined because of you. I told you so."

"Do you know you've said 'I told you so' seventeen times today?" Nate pointed out.

"Eighteen times," Lisa said, "if you count the time I said 'I told—' but was interrupted by Michael Perez calling you a moron."

8

Nate sighed. "Well, at least you didn't call me bad names today."

His classmates had called him party wrecker, jerk, moron, dumbhead, and many other names. Some of the names were so bad they could not even be printed in this book.

"Everyone has probably forgiven you by now," Lisa said as she got off the bus.

Nate followed her.

A tossed tomato followed him and landed splat on his back.

A rotten egg followed the tomato and landed with a splat on the tomato on Nate's back.

"Okay, so maybe they haven't forgiven you," Lisa told Nate.

"I've decided there's only one way out of the trouble I'm in," Nate said. "I have to flee the country."

"Is that all you could come up with?" she asked.

Nate nodded. "In my new country, I'll use a different name."

"Ooh, can I help you pick the name? Please?" Lisa asked. "I think you'd make a good Louie. Or Theodore."

"I was thinking more along the lines of Joe Schmo," Nate said. "I'll also need to wear a disguise at all times."

"Do you want me to draw a mustache and beard on your face with a permanent marker?" Lisa offered as they got to their house.

10

"No thanks." Nate opened the front door.

He asked their mother, "Which country would be best to hide an international fugitive? Or at least an embarrassed fourth grader? Pakistan? Cambodia? And would I look good with my hair dyed blond?"

As usual, their mother stared at the computer monitor in front of her. "That's nice, dear," she said.

"What are you working on?" Lisa asked their mother.

"I'm writing a graphic novel," she said without turning her head. "Graphic novels are very popular now. They're like comic books. They have lots of illustrations, so I don't have to type as many words."

"Mom, I didn't know you could draw," Nate said.

"They're just kids' books. They don't have to be that good," she said. "And I can draw as well as any kid. See?" Their mother stopped staring at the computer long enough to show Nate and Lisa a drawing.

"That's a nice flower," Lisa said.

"I thought it was a pirate skull," Nate said.

"Flower," Lisa said.

"Pirate skull," Nate said.

"Flower," Lisa repeated.

"Pirate skull," Nate repeated.

Their mother laughed. "You kids are so funny, pretending not to know this is a picture of a superhero."

"What superpower does he have?" Nate asked.

"*She* have," Lisa said. "The superhero is obviously a girl."

"He's a boy," Nate argued.

"Girl," Lisa argued.

13

"Boy," Nate said.

"Girl," Lisa said.

"Actually, I haven't figured out whether the superhero should be a boy or a girl," their mother said.

"Well, what superpower does he or she have?" Lisa asked.

Their mother shrugged. "I haven't figured that out either."

"You could make it a supernatural rubber chicken with the ability to give people superpowers," Nate said. He was thinking, of course, of Ed, the rubber chicken. Before their older brother, Dave, left last week to surf the waves on far-off shores, he had given Ed to Nate and Lisa.

Ed wasn't just an ordinary rubber chicken.

14

For one thing, he was much older and much uglier than most rubber chickens. Also, he talked and made jokes, many of them quite corny. Oh, yes, and he also granted superpowers.

"Your idea for a book about a rubber chicken who can give people superpowers is ridiculous," Ms. Zupinski said. "No one would want to read about a supernatural rubber chicken."

Lisa and Nate nodded. "You're probably right, Mom," Lisa said.

"A person would have to be crazy to like a book about a supernatural rubber chicken," Nate added.

"Maybe I should make my hero a superdog," their mother said. "It could be the strongest dog alive, able to stop trains with his bare paws and destroy fifty bad guys with one poisonous bite. He'd even be strong enough to open brand new jars of jelly."

Ms. Zupinski looked down at their dog Plop, who was lying under her chair. "What do you think about that?" she asked the dog.

Plop opened her left eye, then shut it again, and then let out a colossal fart.

"**P.U.!**" Nate screamed.

"EWW!" Lisa yelled.

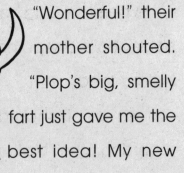

"Wonderful!" their mother shouted. "Plop's big, smelly fart just gave me the best idea! My new

16

book will feature a dog with powerful farts! Hmm, what should I call it? How about Walter? Ooh, I'll call the book *Walter the Farting Dog!* I'm so original!"

Nate and Lisa plugged their noses and ran out of the room. But they couldn't escape the horrible smell.

Chapter 3

Kosher Chicken

Nate stepped into his bedroom and threw his backpack on the floor.

"Be careful!" Ed the supernatural rubber chicken said from on top of Nate's dresser.

Nate tripped over a book on the rug called *Walter the Farting Dog*.

"I told you to be careful," Ed said.

"Don't say 'I told you so,'" Nate said. "I'm tired of hearing that."

"I told you so!" Lisa shouted at Nate from her bedroom.

Nate sat on his bed and put his head in his hands.

"Is something wrong?" Ed asked.

"Not just *something. Everything* is wrong," Nate said. "I'll make a list of the

top five things that went wrong today."

He found a pen and an old report card he'd hidden under his bed, and wrote:

What Went Wrong Today:

1. *No one would play handball with me.*

2. *That bully Hulk Paine stole all the meat from my sandwich, so I had to eat a bread and ketchup sandwich for lunch.*

3. *I accidentally broke Jason Johnson's glasses.*

4. *All the boys in my class are mad at me.*

"Hmm. What should the fifth item be?" Nate wondered.

"Told you so!" Lisa shouted again.

Nate added to the list:

5. *Lisa keeps saying, "I told you so."*

"There, there," the rubber chicken said. "Things aren't so bad. Some people really like ketchup sandwiches. My cousin Phyllis even served them at her bat mitzvah party."

"One of your rubber chicken relatives had a bat mitzvah?" Nate asked.

"I'm one-quarter Jewish, on my mother's side," Ed explained. "Don't worry. Things will get better, Nate."

Nate shook his head. "Once Jason fails the math test and his parents cancel his birthday party, everyone will be even madder at me."

"Good point," Ed said. "Ever thought of leaving the country?"

"Yes, I have," Nate said.

"By the way, what is that horrible smell?"

Ed asked. "At least say 'excuse me' before you stink up the room."

Nate looked up. "That wasn't me," he said. "It was Plop." Then he returned his head to its position in his hands.

"Well? Aren't you going to ask about my day?" Ed asked.

"Sorry," Nate mumbled. "How was your day?"

"My day stunk even before Plop farted," the rubber chicken said. "I've been on your dresser for eight straight hours with nothing to entertain me—no TV, no video games, not even a book."

"You read?" Nate asked.

"Of course I read. What do you think I am? A birdbrain?"

22

Nate didn't answer that.

"Do you have any good books you could put on the dresser for me?" Ed asked. "*Chicken Little*, perhaps?"

"I don't have that one," Nate said.

"*The Little Red Hen*?" the rubber chicken asked.

"I don't have that one either, Ed."

"*Make Way for Ducklings*?" Ed asked.

"Sorry, no." Nate shook his head.

"Don't you have anything for me to read?"

Nate showed Ed the *Walter the Farting Dog* book.

Ed groaned. "No. Yuck."

Nate rummaged through his closet. He dug through mounds of dirty clothes, poker chips, broken snow globes, and his collection of toilet paper rolls. Finally, Nate pulled out a copy of Dr. Seuss's *Fox in Socks*. "How about this book?" he asked Ed.

"**Agh!**" the rubber chicken squawked. "**Get that fox away from me!**"

Nate laughed. "It's just pretend. It's not real."

"That's what you think," Ed said. "People say I'm not real either."

"Well, I know you're real, and I know you can grant wishes," Nate said. "In fact, I need you to grant me a wish."

Lisa walked into the bedroom. "Hi, Ed," she said. "I need you to grant me a wish."

"What bad manners! You didn't even ask me how my day went," the rubber chicken complained.

24

"Sorry," Lisa said. "How was your day?"

"Don't ask," Ed said.

"Okay, great," Lisa said. "Now can you grant my wish?"

"Hey, no fair," Nate told his sister. "It's my turn to ask Ed for a superpower."

"Fighting over me. Don't I feel special?" the rubber chicken said. "Not!"

Nate continued talking. "I broke my friend Jason's glasses. My wish is that he'd get a new pair."

"You can't wish for objects," Ed said. "I only grant requests for superpowers. Duh! And remember, the superpowers last only a day or two."

"Okay, Nate, you had your turn asking for help," Lisa said. "Now it's my turn."

25

"That doesn't count as my turn," Nate protested.

"You said you wanted a turn to ask for help," Lisa said. "You got your turn. It's not my fault that you messed up. Now it's my turn."

Nate crossed his arms. "No way!"

"But I have the greatest idea for a super-power," Lisa said. "I want to make my friend Ashley invisible. That way she can go to Jason's birthday party and spy on the boys and then tell the girls all about it."

"If Jason doesn't pass the math test tomorrow, there won't even be a birthday party," Nate told Lisa. "And I can tell you and the girls what happens at boys' parties. We make fake farts with our underarms, burp the alphabet, and tell underwear jokes."

26

Lisa frowned. "Never mind. You can have your turn, Nate."

"Good," he said. "I figured out what to ask for."

Nate turned to the rubber chicken. "I want you to give my friend Jason super vision. That way, Jason won't need glasses tomorrow and he'll be able to pass the math test."

"Okay," Ed said. "But remember: The first person who touches me will get the superpower. Not counting you and Lisa, of course, because you're my owners. So make sure Jason touches me before anyone else does."

Nate stared at the rubber chicken's black beady eyes, his sharp plastic beak, and his large bumpy stomach and scrawny legs.

27

"Don't worry. I'm sure no one else will want to touch you, Ed. No offense."

"Offense taken!" the rubber chicken said. "For your information, other rubber chickens consider me quite handsome. Did you know I was once mistaken for a rubber swan?" Ed started singing "Way Down Upon the Swanee River," loudly and off-key.

Nate and Lisa plugged their ears.

"I have to go feed my goldfish," Nate said.

"Me too," Lisa said.

Ed stopped singing long enough to say, "But you don't own any goldfish."

"Our imaginary goldfish," Nate said.

"They eat a lot of imaginary food," Lisa added.

She and Nate rushed out of the room.

Chapter 4

Thick Cement Walls
Can Be Evil

"I can't wait for Jason to get super vision! This is great!" Nate exclaimed as he walked with Lisa and Ed toward the school playground.

"I can't wait to get out of your backpack! This is terrible!" Ed exclaimed to Nate as he got bumped around. "The smell is killing me. What's in here, anyway?"

"Nothing that would smell bad." Nate shrugged. "Just my lunch, a dog biscuit I found in the sewer last year, half of a tuna fish

29

sandwich left over from kindergarten, and a pair of socks."

"Moldy, mildewy socks," the rubber chicken said.

Lisa wrinkled her nose. "EWW."

"The odor inside this backpack is almost as bad as your teacher's," Ed said.

Nate shook his head. "No odor even comes close to the stink of Mrs. Crabpit—except the smell of Plop's farts."

Lisa pointed to the playground. "There's your friend Jason Johnson."

"Awesome!" Nate said. "Once Jason touches Ed, he'll have great eyesight. And with great eyesight, Jason might pass the math test and get to have his birthday party."

"Do me a favor," the rubber chicken said.

30

"Throw out everything in your backpack except for your lunch and me. If I have to spend any more time smelling the stinky stuff in here, I may pass out. And I can't grant superpowers if I'm passed out."

Nate shrugged. "It smells fine to me. I like the scent of rotting tuna fish mixed with mold, mildew, and sewer water."

"EWW!" Lisa said again.

"Mmm!" Nate said. "But if you insist, I'll throw away some stuff."

"I insist," the rubber chicken said.

Nate stopped near a garbage can on the playground, took off his backpack, unzipped it, and reached his hand into it.

"Be careful of my delicate face!" Ed cried.

"Sorry." Nate pulled out the sandwich left

31

over from kindergarten. "Looks like there are a few worms on this. I wonder if it's still good enough to eat."

"Eww! Dump it immediately," Lisa told him.

Nate tossed the sandwich and its worms into the trash. "Okay, all done."

"Wait!" Ed shouted. "You've got other disgusting things in here, like an old dog biscuit and filthy socks."

"I can't throw those away! I may need them one day," Nate told the rubber chicken. "Now, let's get Jason to touch you before school starts."

"Whatever you do," Lisa told Nate, "make sure no one touches Ed before your friend Jason does."

"Don't worry," Nate said.

"Do you want my help?" Lisa offered.

Nate shook his head. "I don't need your help." Then he shouted, "Jason! I want to show you something cool!"

Jason walked over with his arms stretched out ahead of him. "Nate, is that you?" he asked. "I can't see."

Jason sniffed the air. "That's definitely Nate's backpack. I can tell by the stink. The only thing worse than the smell of that backpack is the smell of Mrs. Crabpit."

"You obviously haven't smelled our dog Plop's farts," Lisa said.

Nate said, "I have something special to show you, Jason."

Jason shook his head. "You can't show me anything because I can't see."

33

"Right," Nate said. "I meant I want you to touch it."

He took the rubber chicken out of the backpack.

Ed yelled, "It's about time! Ten more minutes in there and the odor would have killed me!"

Nate and Lisa ignored the rubber chicken's complaints. They were the only people who could hear him.

Nate put Ed in front of Jason. "Feel this," he said.

Just as Jason reached out his hand, Hulk Paine walked in front of him.

Jason accidentally touched Hulk's stomach instead of the rubber chicken. "That feels like a thick cement wall," Jason said. "Why do you want me to touch a wall, Nate?"

"Who's calling me a wall?" Hulk shouted. "And no one touches the Hulk without prior written permission."

He picked up Jason by the back of his shirt and hurled him into the garbage can. "I hope that will teach you a lesson," he said.

Chapter 5

And Ed Thought Nate's Backpack Smelled Bad

Jason yelled from inside the trash can, "That was one dirty trick you played on me, Nate! First you broke my glasses. Then, when I could barely see, you fooled me into making Hulk Paine mad at me."

"That sounds like two dirty tricks to me," the rubber chicken said.

"Shut up," Nate told Ed.

"And now you're telling me to shut up," Jason complained. **"Only jerks say 'shut up!'"**

36

"It's not nice to say 'shut up,' " Lisa said.

"I'm sorr—" Before Nate could say he was sorry, Jason interrupted him. "You're a big jerk, Nate Zupinski!"

A crowd formed. "Nate's a big jerk," Michael Perez said.

"Nate used to be nice, but now he's a big jerk," Dan the Dawdler said.

"Yeah, what *he* said," Grant Sinker said.

"Ditto," Jason Johnson said.

"Exactly," Michael Perez said.

The boys helped Jason out of the trash can. Worms, mold, and old tuna fish clung to Jason. And he still hadn't touched the rubber chicken.

At least no one else had either. Nate had promised Lisa that the chicken wouldn't fall

into the wrong hands. He didn't want her saying "I told you so."

Suddenly, a terrible odor came upon them.

That terrible odor meant only one thing.

Sure enough, Mrs. Crabpit appeared. "Stop playing with the trash or you'll get smelly," she told Jason.

Then she took the rubber chicken out of Nate's hands. "And you shouldn't be playing with trash either," she told Nate.

Mrs. Crabpit threw the rubber chicken into the garbage can.

"**Agh!**" Ed screamed. "**Get me out of here!**"

Nate and Lisa bent over the garbage can to save him.

"I told you kids not to play with the trash!" Mrs. Crabpit yelled. "Now get to class. You have a math test today."

Nate and Lisa looked back at Ed and mouthed, "Sorry."

"Sorry? Sorry? Is that all you have to say for yourselves?" Ed complained. "I tried to help you and your friend Jason. But what do I get for my trouble? I get bumped around in Nate's stinky backpack, thrown through the air by Mrs. Crabpit, and left in this disgusting

39

garbage can. Yuck! There are worms on me! And tuna fish. And mold. Help! Nate! Lisa! Please!"

But they couldn't help the rubber chicken. They had to follow Mrs. Crabpit to the classroom.

Now Nate's friends were even angrier at him, and Ed was stuck in the garbage can. Could Nate's life get any worse?

"Wow," Mrs. Crabpit said. "I can see everything more clearly all of a sudden."

Oh no.

Nate remembered that Mrs. Crabpit had touched the rubber chicken.

"My vision has really improved," Mrs. Crabpit said.

Yikes! She had gotten super vision.

40

Nate had a feeling that his life was going to get worse—a lot worse.

Lisa shook her head. "I *told* you not to let the wrong person touch the rubber chicken," she said. **"Told you so."**

Yep. Nate's life had gotten a lot worse.

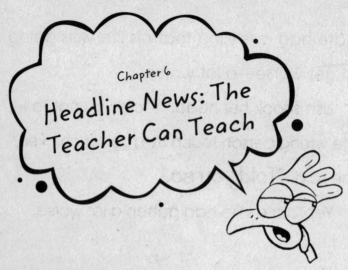

Chapter 6
Headline News: The Teacher Can Teach

With her new super vision, Mrs. Crabpit could see the slightest problems.

She also could see things that weren't problems, not even in the slightest, except to a teacher with super vision.

For instance, when the class read their science books, Mrs. Crabpit couldn't believe that no one knew how many spots were on the one-inch picture of the dalmation.

"There are 138 spots!" she screamed. "It's

so obvious!" Then she pointed at the open book on Nate's desk. "What is that?"

"Just my science book," he said.

She marched over. "No, I meant the book inside your science book." She pulled out a comic book.

Then she peered at Lisa on the other side of the room. "You're supposed to be taking notes," Mrs. Crabpit told her, "not drawing

THERE ARE 138 SPOTS! IT'S SO OBVIOUS!

pretty pictures of a lily, three roses, seven dandelions, and forty-six blades of grass."

Next, she pointed at Benny B. Benjamin. "You are not looking at your textbook and taking notes. You are looking at Ashley Chang and drawing hearts."

"Really?" Ashley's face flushed with hope.

"Really." Benny's face flushed with embarrassment.

"Because of the class's poor behavior," Mrs. Crabpit said, "I will cancel the movie scheduled for today."

Everyone groaned.

Lisa raised her hand. "Could you spend the extra time helping us prepare for the math test?"

Everyone groaned again.

Well, not everyone groaned. Mrs. Crabpit smiled. "It delights me that you want to learn. But make sure you're paying attention. I'll be watching you very closely."

Then she taught the class math. Because they couldn't get away with looking at other things today, everyone was forced to concentrate on the lesson.

Dan the Dawdler even got around to opening his math book.

Ashley Chang even answered a few questions. She even got the answers right.

Jason Johnson even said, "I finally understand this stuff. I would have a chance of passing the math test if I could see."

Lisa had never realized that Mrs. Crabpit could actually teach them something, or

45

that she could actually learn something.

Maybe Mrs. Crabpit is an okay teacher after all, Lisa thought. *Aside from her horrific smell, of course.*

Then Mrs. Crabpit pointed to Benny B. Benjamin's shoe. "You're wiggling your toe!" she yelled. "Stop disrupting my class."

Next, Mrs. Crabpit pounded on Lisa's desk. "The bottom of your desk is filthy! I see a pencil mark on it," the teacher said. "No recess for you today, Lisa Zupinski. Instead, you will stay in the classroom and wipe down the bottom of your desk."

So Mrs. Crabpit wasn't an okay teacher after all. It was a nice thought while it lasted, though. Lisa glared at Nate and mouthed, "I told you so."

"And Lisa, clean the bottom of everyone else's desks too. I've never seen such a big mess before," the teacher said. She obviously had never seen the inside of Nate's backpack.

Lisa sighed. Mrs. Crabpit's super vision could last two days. Lisa didn't think she could take another minute of it.

Chapter 7

Super Lisa to the Rescue

When the bell rang for recess, everyone but Lisa ran out of the classroom. Today, they were not only fleeing Mrs. Crabpit's bad odor, but also her super vision.

Lisa went to the classroom sink, wet some paper towels, and started cleaning the desk bottoms.

"I never noticed how messy this classroom was," Mrs. Crabpit said.

"It's eye opening, isn't it?" Lisa said.

"To teach the class some discipline, I will make today's math test extra hard."

Lisa cleared her throat. "But if we know we can't pass the test, we won't try to learn. We'll return to our old ways of not paying attention."

"What do you mean?" the teacher asked.

"Well, for the last math test? The one about seven trains, a car, a bike, a scooter, and a unicycle going eleven different directions at eight different speeds?"

"Nine different speeds." Mrs. Crabpit rubbed her hands with glee. "Oh, that was a real challenge!"

"Too much of a challenge," Lisa said as she cleaned the windowsills. "We knew we could never figure out the answers, so we didn't even try. Nate answered with the uniform numbers of his favorite football players. I used the heights and weights of my favorite dolls. Dan the Dawdler complained that he had time only to put his name on the top of his paper. Actually, he only had time to write 'Da.' "

"Oh, I thought there was a new student in the class named Da," Mrs. Crabpit said.

Lisa looked at her teacher with her most pitiful expression. "So, do you think you could give us a math test that we have a chance at passing?"

Mrs. Crabpit sighed.

Her stinky breath blew right into the cage of the class gerbil, Poopie, who fainted.

"All right, I'll make the math test easier,"

Mrs. Crabpit told Lisa. "Meanwhile, clean the windowsills."

"But I just cleaned them," Lisa said.

"They're filthy!" She pointed. "I see two specks of dust on them."

"I can't see the dust," Lisa said. "May I have a magnifying glass to help me?"

Mrs. Crabpit gave Lisa a magnifying glass. Then Lisa cleaned the windowsills and the blinds and the doorknob and the sink and about a zillion other things.

As the bell rang to signal that recess was over, Lisa put the magnifying glass on top of Jason Johnson's desk and smiled.

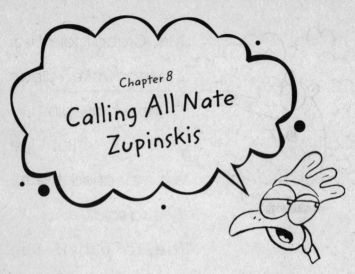

Chapter 8

Calling All Nate Zupinskis

Once Nate got on the playground, he almost wished he were back in the classroom. At least Lisa got to suffer in silence. Nate was surrounded by angry kids.

"Soon Mrs. Crabpit will be giving the math test, and Jason can't see a thing," Michael Perez said.

"Yeah. He'll fail the test and won't get to have a birthday party," Dan the Dawdler said.

"Yeah, what *he* said," Grant Sinker said.

"Ditto," Jason Johnson said.

"Exactly," Michael Perez said.

"Okay, I get it. You're mad at me," Nate said.

"And we think you're a jerk," Michael said.

"Yeah, a really bad jerk," Dan said.

"Yeah, what *he* said," Grant said.

"Ditto," Jason said.

"Exactly," Michael said.

"I could try to help Jason study for the math test," Nate offered.

"Without my glasses?" Jason shook his head. "All the studying in the world won't help me without my glasses."

"I'd be happy to throw Nate into the trash can," Hulk Paine offered.

Luckily—for Nate, but not for Hulk—the

lunch monitor came by. "Nate Zupinski, go to the principal's office," she said.

"Me?" Nate asked.

"How many Nate Zupinskis are there?" she said.

Actually, there are three other Nate Zupinskis: an accountant in Cleveland, Ohio; a poet in Poland; and a busboy in Chattanooga, Tennessee. But Nate and the lunch monitor didn't know about the other Nate Zupinskis.

"What's wrong?" Nate asked.

The lunch monitor shrugged. "Family emergency."

Nate rushed to the principal's office.

Chapter 9
Surferdude 911

When Nate got to the principal's office, he found his older brother Dave there, sound asleep.

Nate shook him. "What's wrong? Is it Mom?"

"No, it's me, Dave, your brother." Dave pointed to himself. "If you think I'm Mom, then I need a haircut."

"What are you doing here? I thought you were surfing in Malibu," Nate said.

"Dude, I missed you and Lisa and Mom. But most of all I missed Ed, the supernatural rubber chicken." Dave swiped at his wet eyes. "I just have to see him and give him a hug. Where is the cute little dude?"

"I wouldn't call him cute, but—" Nate slapped his palm over his forehead. "I forgot about him."

Dave shook his head. "I gave Ed to you and Lisa so you'd take care of him, not treat him like a piece of trash."

"Sorry," Nate said.

"So where is he?" Dave asked.

"In the trash can," Nate said.

They ran out of the office.

Dave's cell phone rang on the way. He stopped.

Nate waited for him.

Then Dave ran toward the parking lot.

"Are you leaving?" Nate asked.

"I wish I could stay but the waves are calling me," Dave said. "Actually, my friends are calling me, saying the waves are calling them."

"I thought you had to see the rubber chicken and give him a hug," Nate said.

"Gotta go surf." Dave ran to his truck, shouted, **"Hang ten!"** gave his surfboard a hug, and drove away.

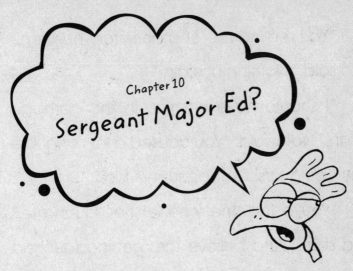

Chapter 10

Sergeant Major Ed?

Nate went to look for the rubber chicken.

He found him, still in the garbage can. Ed was covered with string cheese, carrot sticks, hard-boiled eggs, apple slices, and other healthy snacks that parents packed and kids threw right into the garbage can.

Ed yelled, "What are you waiting for, you nincompoop? Get me out of here!"

Nate quickly reached into the trash and pulled Ed out.

"You remind me of a one-story building," Ed said. "Nothing upstairs."

"I should have left you in the garbage can," Nate said. "You caused a lot of trouble by giving Mrs. Crabpit super vision."

"You're the one who let her touch me," Ed said. "And believe me, getting touched by Mrs. Crabpit was one of the worst experiences of my life. It was almost as terrible as serving in Iraq in '04."

"You fought in Iraq?" Nate asked.

"I gave a few soldiers super strength when they needed it most." Ed blinked back tears. "Though most of them were already super strong without me."

Nate hugged Ed. "You may be ugly and rubbery on the outside, but on the inside you're one sensitive little guy."

"Are you talking to a rubber chicken?"
Michael Perez asked.

Nate had forgotten that there were
people around, and that he and Lisa were
the only ones who could hear the rubber
chicken speak.

"Weirdo," Michael said.

"Party-spoiling rubber-chicken hugger,"
Dan the Dawdler said.

"Yeah, what *he* said," Grant Sinker said.

"Ditto," Jason Johnson said.

"Exactly," Michael said.

"This week keeps getting worse and worse," Nate said.

"Sometimes things don't seem to be working out," the rubber chicken told him, "but they really do in the end."

"Oh, shut up," Nate said.

"It's not nice to say shut—" Ed started to say.

Before Ed could finish talking, Nate put him in his backpack and zipped it closed.

Chapter 11
Supernatural Chopped Liver

"Psst! Nate!" the rubber chicken whispered from inside Nate's backpack.

"Don't bother me. I'm in a bad mood," Nate said.

"*You're* in a bad mood?" the chicken asked. "Try spending half the day in a garbage can and the other half in a stinky backpack. If you let me out of your backpack, I'll give you some advice."

"Good advice?" Nate asked.

"No. Bad advice," Ed said. **"Duh!"**

Nate took the rubber chicken out of his backpack. "Okay, what's your advice?"

"Your teacher has super vision, right?" Ed said.

"You're the one who gave it to her. **Duh!**"

"It was *your* wish," Ed said.

"Whatever," Nate said. "She has super vision."

"So why don't you write a note in class for her to see?"

"You call that good advice?" Nate rolled his eyes. "I'll get in trouble!"

"Not if you write a nice note," Ed said. "A nice note about Mrs. Crabpit. A nice note about Mrs. Crabpit being your favorite teacher."

64

"She's my *least* favorite teacher," Nate said. "She's everyone's least favorite teacher. She's the worst teacher in the whole entire school, in the whole entire country, in the whole entire world, in the whole entire universe, in the—"

"All right, all right. I get your point," Ed said. "But here's *my* point. You write a *fake* note, *pretending* she's your favorite teacher. Then she sees the note, thinks you're a great kid, gets in a good mood, and celebrates by canceling the math test."

Nate thought about Ed's plan. Then he asked, "But what if Mrs. Crabpit celebrates by giving us an extra-hard math test?"

"Then she might give you a good grade on it, at least," Ed said.

65

Nate shook his head. "But that won't help Jason do well on the test."

The chicken sighed. "I try to help you, but all you do is peck at my ideas like they're chicken feed."

"Your ideas are for the birds," Nate said.

"I got it!" Ed exclaimed. "You sign the note from both you and Jason. Then the teacher will like both of you."

"Now you're talking!" Nate said.

"You mean, 'Now I'm squawking,' " Ed squawked.

"That too. It's a great idea. It could solve all my problems!" Nate shouted.

Jason walked over. "What are you so happy about? Is it that you broke my glasses and got me thrown into the garbage can and ruined the best birthday party ever?"

Nate shook his head. "None of the above. I just thought of a great way for you to pass the math test."

"*You* thought of it?" Ed complained. "What am I, chopped liver?"

"Okay, I can't take full credit for the idea," Nate said.

"*Full* credit?" Ed said. "You can barely take partial credit."

Just as Jason asked Nate what he was talking about, Nate told Ed to shut up.

"You really are a jerk," Jason told Nate.

"I didn't mean for *you* to shut up," Nate said.

"It's not nice to say 'shut up' to anyone," Jason said.

67

"Sorry," Nate told him. "Anyway, listen to my plan."

"*My* plan," Ed said.

Nate ignored him. He told Jason, "I'm going to write a note about how much we like Mrs. Crabpit. Mrs. Crabpit will find the note. She'll be so happy, she'll either cancel the math test or give us great grades on it."

Jason wrinkled his forehead. "Hmm, that might actually work. Maybe you're not such a big, dumb jerk after all."

"Thanks," Nate said. "That's the nicest thing anyone's said to me all day."

Jason pointed to Ed. "That rubber chicken of yours was better off in the garbage can. Even without my glasses, I can tell that thing is ugly!"

"Oh yeah?" Ed squawked. "If I had a face like yours, I'd walk backward."

Nate threw the rubber chicken into his backpack.

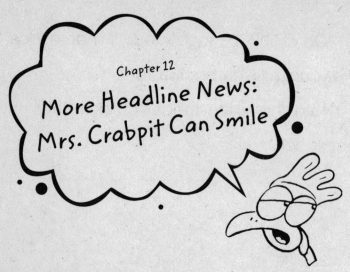

Chapter 12

More Headline News:
Mrs. Crabpit Can Smile

When recess ended, Nate was the first student back in the classroom—

Except for Lisa, of course. She whispered, "I think I fixed your problems."

Nate ignored her.

He knew Lisa couldn't help.

He rushed to his seat and started writing the note.

Dear Principal Pal,

~~I am writing about my~~ We are writing about our
teacher, Mrs. Crabpit. She is ~~awful~~ awesome.

We hope that our ~~stinkiest~~ favorite teacher gives
us a math test we can ~~survive~~ pass, because we want
to show our gratitude for her. ~~And also because~~
~~Jason has this great birthday party planned, and all~~
~~the boys hate me now.~~

~~In~~sincerely,

Your ~~buttkisser~~ students,
    ~~Nate~~ Nathan Zupinski

71

He wasn't able to write "and Jason Johnson." Long yellow nails on the long, bent fingers of Mrs. Crabpit's long, smelly hand clawed at the note before he could finish it.

"Nathan Zupinski, how dare you write notes in class!" Mrs. Crabpit exclaimed. "This calls for a suspension. And a meeting with your parents, and me, and the principal. What do you have to say for yourself, young man?"

He opened his mouth to talk, but no words came out.

Mrs. Crabpit's frown grew so large it nearly ran off her face. "Well?" she screeched.

Nate finally managed to utter, "Rea . . . re a . . . read the note."

She held it up to her frown of a face.

She started to read it.

72

As she read, her frown got smaller and smaller.

By the time she finished reading the note, her frown had turned into a smile.

She pressed the note against her heart and said, "Natey! I'm all aflutter now!"

Nate supposed that was a good thing. But he hated being called "Natey." Also, he

73

was a bit worried about Mrs. Crabpit being all aflutter, since he didn't know what that meant.

"I'm going to call Principal Pal right now," she said.

Nate gulped. "You're going to call the principal?"

"You betcha, Natey. But before I do, I want everyone to wash their hands and faces. Ashley Chang, you have a speck of dust on your pinky finger. Jason Johnson, you have a hair out of place on your head. And Grant Sinker, you have a pretzel crumb under your shoe. What a motley group of students!" She smiled at Nate. "Except for Natey, of course."

She banged her hand on Nate's desk. "Everyone get to the sink and wash up!

What are you waiting for? Move it, move it, move it!"

So they rushed to the sink. Hulk Paine pushed his way to the front and Dan the Dawdler shuffled his way toward the back.

Mrs. Crabpit called the principal. "Get to my classroom!" she yelled into the phone. "And make it snappy. I need to talk to you about Nathan Zupinski."

Nate told himself not to be nervous.

It didn't work.

When it was his turn at the sink, he splashed water on his face.

That didn't work either. The water got on his pants.

"It looks like Nate Zupinski just had a potty accident," Michael Perez said.

"Why didn't you use the bathroom during recess?" Dan the Dawdler asked.

"Yeah, what *he* said," Grant Sinker said.

"Ditto," Jason Johnson said.

"Exactly," Michael Perez said.

Nate soaked his head.

Chapter 13

Mrs. Crabpit Stings Like a Bee

Nate heard footsteps running toward the classroom. The footsteps stopped completely a few feet from the door.

Mrs. Crabpit rushed to the door and flung it open.

Principal Pal took a big step back. He nibbled on his thumbnail.

"It's about time," Mrs. Crabpit snapped at him.

"M-may I help you?" the principal stuttered.

"You think *you* can help *me*?" Mrs. Crapbit asked. "When has that ever happened?"

His forehead wrinkled. "Well, Mrs. Crapbit, if I recall, seven and a half years ago—"

"Never mind," she said. "Look at this." She handed him the note.

He read it, then peered at the kids in the classroom. "Who is Nathan Zupinski?" he asked in a stern voice.

Nate swallowed.

Then he swallowed again.

Then he swallowed one more time.

Make that two more times.

Okay, three more times.

After all that swallowing, his throat was killing him.

Finally, he put his hand up about half an

inch and whispered, "Nathan Zupinski. That would be me."

Principal Pal walked over to Nate and said, "I'm glad you like your teacher."

"Like me? He loves me!" Mrs. Crabpit gave herself a big hug. "Of course, how could anyone *not* love me?"

"Easily," Lisa whispered.

Nate started making a list in his head.

What I Don't Love About Mrs. Crabpit

1. Her bad breath
2. Her hard tests
3. Her awful smell
4. Her screechy voice
5. Her

"I don't find Mrs. Crabpit loveable at all." Ed interrupted Nate's thoughts. "I wish she'd make like a tree and leave."

"Yeah. Mrs. Crabpit should make like a bee and buzz off," Nate said.

"What?" Mrs. Crabpit asked.

Nate clapped his hand over his mouth. "I was saying, uh, I wish you'd fly like a bee, so you could pollinate students and teachers everywhere with your wisdom."

Mrs. Crabpit stuck her finger in the air. "Hey! Natey's just given me a wonderful idea! I should train all the other teachers at school so they can be just like me."

"Jerk!" everyone except Dan the Dawdler whispered to Nate.

"You'd love it if all the teachers were just

like me. Wouldn't you, Natey?" Mrs. Crabpit asked.

Nate nodded. Really, though, he'd love that as much as he loved brussels sprout-spinach casserole.

"Jerk!" Dan the Dawdler whispered to Nate.

"The other teachers don't challenge these poor children like I do," Mrs. Crabpit told the principal. "My students might complain, but I know they secretly love a good challenge."

Nate didn't love a good challenge, secretly or otherwise. He didn't think there was such a thing as a good challenge. But he kept nodding his head.

"Just for you, Natey," Mrs. Crabpit said, "I'm going to make today's math test extra challenging—so challenging that it will be almost impossible to pass." She rubbed her palms together. "Your sister had talked me into making the math test easier, but you just changed my mind."

Then she turned to Principal Pal. "What are you still doing here? I've got an extremely hard math test to give. **So beat it!**"

"Yes, ma'am," he said as he ran out the door.

"Everyone, take out your pencils and papers," Mrs. Crabpit ordered. "And you'll need plenty of erasers."

Then she shrieked, **"Question One. There are thirteen trains. One travels eighteen miles per hour from the southeast. The second one goes** forty-nine miles per minute from the northeast. The third train runs 103.72 miles per day from Nova Scotia . . ."

Amazingly, Nate was able to figure out the answer. The studying he'd done today in class had helped him. The test was extra challenging, but for the first time this year, he felt up to the challenge.

After the students turned in their tests, Nate looked around the classroom. Everyone was smiling as if they were all up to the challenge too. Well, Hulk Paine wasn't smiling, but he never smiled.

Soon, everyone put their heads on their desks in exhaustion. Jason Johnson fell asleep with his mouth open. A fly flew in and dropped her eggs on his tongue.

"That was fun!" Mrs. Crabpit squealed. "There's nothing more exciting than a challenging math test!"

Nate thought of many things more exciting than a challenging math test.

Things More Exciting Than a Challenging Math Test

1. Finishing a challenging math test

2. Disneyland

3. Halloween

4. Long car rides

5. Brushing my teeth

6. Watching paint dry

7. Getting beat up by everyone who wanted to go to Jason Johnson's birthday party

The lunch bell rang. Nate hoped the boys wouldn't beat him up too badly.

"I knew I should have moved to another country," he said to himself.

Chapter 14
Super Jerk

Jason Johnson was very thirsty. His tongue felt thick. He didn't know that a fly had dropped her eggs in his mouth.

At lunchtime, he stopped at the drinking fountain. The water felt weird going down his throat, and he thought he heard a tiny buzzing noise.

He walked over to where Nate was sitting. **"You jerk!"** Jason yelled. Three baby flies flew out of his mouth. "You told me the note about Mrs. Crabpit was supposed to be from both of us."

"Mrs. Crabpit saw the note before I could sign your name," Nate said.

"Oh, sure. Anyway, you're still a jerk for breaking my glasses," Jason said. "Also, for getting Mrs. Crabpit to make the math test harder. And for not signing my name to the note. So that makes you a triple jerk."

"Yeah, a triple jerk," Michael said behind Jason.

"And you ruined Jason's birthday party," Grant said behind Michael. "So that makes you a quadruple jerk."

Jason, Michael, and Grant stomped off to a different table, leaving Nate to eat lunch by himself.

Lisa came by and asked her brother, "You want company?"

Nate shook his head.

"Hey, buddy," Ed said from inside Nate's backpack, "I'll keep you company."

Nate sighed. "No. Thanks anyway."

"Let me out of this smelly backpack," Ed demanded.

"No. I'm still mad at you for telling me to write that dumb note," Nate said.

"Quintuple jerk!" Ed yelled.

Lisa put her hand on Nate's shoulder. "I've been trying to help you," she said. "Before you wrote that note, I had convinced Mrs.

Crabpit to make the math test easier."

"Well, it was really hard. And without his glasses, I'm sure Jason Johnson failed."

"What if he used a magnifying glass?" Lisa asked.

"Oh, sure. Where would he get that?"

"Well, when I was—"

"Lisa," Nate interrupted her. "Just leave me alone."

"But, I—"

He cut her off again. "You're not helping me at all. Good-bye."

Chapter 15

If You're Happy and You Know It, Stand on a Chair

After lunch, Mrs. Crabpit handed back the math tests. There was a big red B on Lisa's test. However, the B was crossed off and a big red C was substituted for it. Next to the grade, Mrs. Crabpit wrote: Points taken off for missing a dust mite today when you were cleaning.

There was a big red C on Nate's test. However, the C was crossed off and a big red B substituted for it. Next to the grades, Mrs. Crabpit wrote:

Extra credit given for writing a note in class.

As Mrs. Crabpit got near Jason, Nate hoped there were enough tissues in the classroom to handle all of Jason's tears that would fall after he saw his test grade.

More importantly, Nate hoped no one would beat him up after school.

Mrs. Crabpit frowned as she returned the test to Jason.

Jason jumped on top of his chair and screamed, "Yahoo! A D minus! I passed the math test! Having that magnifying glass really helped. And studying probably helped a little too."

"Nate, I told you I gave Jason a magnifying glass," Lisa said. **"Told–"**

Before Lisa could finish saying "Told you so,"

all the boys in the classroom stood on their chairs and burst into cheers and applause.

Well, Dan the Dawdler didn't because he was a dawdler.

"Class! Class!" Mrs. Crabpit yelled. "Sit down and stop clapping and looking so happy. Put those frowns back on your faces this instant!"

But for once, the boys were much too excited to listen to her.

Suddenly, the door opened and Principal Pal burst in.

"Six different teachers just called to complain about the noise in here," he said. "You're disturbing the other classes."

The boys kept on clapping and cheering from atop their chairs.

Dan the Dawdler finally joined them.

"Mrs. Crabpit, you need to **QUIET YOUR CLASS!**" the principal yelled.

"Boys! Boys! **SHUT UP!**" she screamed.

93

"It's not nice to say 'shut up,' " Lisa said.

No one heard her because the boys were still clapping and cheering.

Principal Pal crossed his arms. "Mrs. Crabpit, you can't train the other teachers to act just like you if you can't even control your own class."

After hearing that, the boys clapped and cheered even harder.

The girls joined in too.

Even the rubber chicken clucked his hardest.

And Poopie, the class gerbil, woke up and squealed, "Ee ee ee!" (In gerbil language, this means, "I'm so happy, I'm going to poop in every corner of my cage today.")

The loud noises didn't stop. Not when Mrs. Crabpit screamed even louder, not when

94

the bell rang, and not even after everyone rushed out of the classroom.

They ran to the front of school, still clapping and cheering.

"See you guys tomorrow at my birthday party!" Jason yelled.

"Me too?" Nate asked.

"Of course," Jason said. "I forgive you."

"Me too?" Lisa asked.

"Yuck. No girls allowed!" Jason yelled.

Nate raced to the school bus stop.

Ed screamed from inside the backpack, "Slow down! I'm getting tossed and turned like crazy! Backpacks should not be used as blenders!"

But Nate couldn't hear him because he was chanting, "Party! Party! Party!"

95

Chapter 16
Tickle Me Edmo

"Ow! You're killing me!" Ed screamed in the bathtub.

"Don't exaggerate," Lisa said. "You have about a thousand tons of dirt behind your ears. I need to clean them with my pretty pink washcloth."

"That's not just dirt you're scrubbing off. It's half my scalp," Ed complained.

"Don't you want to look nice for Jason Johnson's birthday party today?" Lisa asked.

He sighed. "I guess."

"Oh, good," Lisa said, "because I just love giving baths. And I'm tired of bathing my Peepee Patsy doll. She keeps having potty accidents in the tub and making me start all over again."

"Are you done yet?" the rubber chicken asked. "I'm getting waterlogged."

"Once you see yourself in the mirror looking all shiny and sweet, you'll thank me," Lisa said.

"I highly doubt that." Ed rolled his eyes. "Hurry up. I don't want to miss the birthday party."

Lisa checked her pink polka-dot watch. "Ooh, time flies when you're having fun. We'd better hurry." She unplugged the drain, rinsed Ed, and wrapped him in a pastel pink towel.

Then she bent down and took a deep whiff of him. "Mmm. You smell like strawberries."

"I smell like a girl," Ed complained. "Just bring me to Nate's room. Maybe the bad odor in there will rub off on me."

Lisa shook her head. "You can't go to the party like that."

"What do you mean?" Ed asked.

"I still need to fluff your Hawaiian lei, gloss your beak, plump your feathers, and buff your claws." She clapped her hands. "Ooh, I haven't had this much fun since I gave my dolls hair extensions!"

Ed sighed again. "Why me?"

Lisa tickled him under his chin.

She had just finished tying Ed's Hawaiian lei into a bow tie when Nate walked into the bathroom.

"I wanted to say good-bye before I leave for Jason Johnson's party," Nate said. "So good-bye."

"Wait!" the rubber chicken called out. "I just let Lisa scrub me in the bath and shampoo my rubber feathers."

Nate winced. "You like that sort of thing?"

99

"Are you kidding? I hate it!" Ed said. "But I wanted to look good for the party."

"What party?" Nate asked.

"Did you just fall off the dumb truck? Jason's birthday party. We'd better get going."

"*We?* Where's *your* invitation?" Nate asked.

"I've been looking forward to this party for so long." Ed's voice trembled. "Please, Nate?"

"Okay. I'll take you to the party. But try not to embarrass me," Nate said. "Let's go."

"Can I go too?" Lisa asked.

"No," Nate said.

"But there's something I need to tell you about the party," Lisa said.

"No girls allowed," Ed said. He and Nate left the room.

Lisa picked up the bathroom phone and called her best friend, Ashley. "We have to move forward with our plan," Lisa told her. "Otherwise, Jason Johnson's birthday party will be a total disaster."

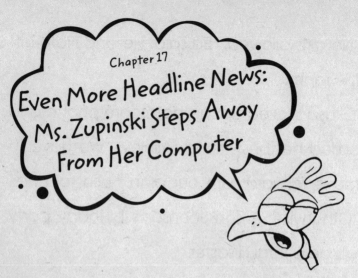

Chapter 17
Even More Headline News: Ms. Zupinski Steps Away From Her Computer

With Ed in his arms, Nate went to find his mother.

She was at the computer, as usual.

"Mom?"

"Hmm," she said as she typed.

"Remember that party I told you I needed a ride to?"

"You did?" Ms. Zupinski kept typing.

"I told you six times today and eight times yesterday and—"

"Told me what?" Ms. Zupinski asked.

Nate forced back a scream that was trying to escape from the back of his mouth. "My friend Jason is having a birthday party and I need a ride," he told his mother.

"Oh." She shrugged. "Why didn't you tell me?"

"So can you drive me over to Jason's house?" Nate asked.

His mother sighed. "I guess. I wish you'd told me earlier."

"Did you remember to get Jason a present, by any chance?" Nate said. "I asked you eleven times."

"I've got the perfect present!" she exclaimed.

Now Nate sighed.

His mother grabbed two of the children's books she'd written: *Spot and Rover Rest in Peace* and *Snookums: The Dog Who Rescued Little Larry but Then Was Mangled to Death*. She put the books in a plastic bag, along with her new manuscript, *Walter the Farting Superhero Dog*.

"That's the entire present?" Nate asked.

"Oh, sorry," Ms. Zupinski said. "I forgot the best part."

"A gift certificate to a video game store?" Nate asked her.

"No." She took out a pen and autographed the books. "Jacob's going to love these," she said.

"It's Jason."

"Oops. I signed the books 'To Jared.' "

A bit of scream escaped from Nate's mouth before he could stop it.

"What's that noise?" his mother asked

"A burp," Nate lied. "Excuse me. By the way, did you happen to buy Jason a card?"

His mother handed him a marker. "Just write 'Happy birthday, Jaden. Love, Nate' on the plastic bag."

Nate wrote "Happy birthday, Jason. From, Nate" on the bag because he thought writing "love" would lead to torment and suffering. Also, he didn't know anyone named Jaden.

He walked to the car with Ed and the birthday gifts.

His mother trailed behind.

Lisa was already in the back seat.

"I need to tell you two things," Nate said

to Lisa. "One, Jason's birthday party is just for boys. And two, you're not a boy."

"I know that," Lisa said. "But—"

"We need to hurry," their mother urged. "I just thought of a brilliant idea for a new graphic novel, and I want to rush back to my computer to type it up and scribble some cute pictures."

"Another brilliant idea?" Lisa rolled her eyes.

"Lisa, you'd better not show up at Jason's party," Nate said as he got into the car.

"But I—"

Ms. Zupinski interrupted Lisa again. "Don't you want to hear about my brilliant idea?" she asked as she drove away.

"Not really," Nate and Lisa muttered.

"Okay, okay. Since you insist, I'll tell you," their mother said. "I'm going to write about a girl who lives on a farm in a small state— maybe Kansas. A tornado blows her to a strange land. To find her way home, she'll have to fight off an evil witch and flying monkeys. Ooh, I love it!"

"You could name the main character Dorothy," Lisa said.

"Dorothy? Yes! Great name!" their mother said. "And of course, I'll put a dog in my book. I can draw a nice picture of a dog. Sometimes, people can even figure out that the drawing is of a dog."

She talked about her new idea during the entire ride to the party.

Meanwhile, Ed hummed "Somewhere

Over the Rainbow" and "We're off to See the Wizard."

When they arrived at Jason's house, Lisa got out of the car.

"You're not going to the party, are you?" Nate asked her.

"Well, I—"

Nate interrupted her. "You can't come. No girls allowed."

"But—"

"Get out of here." Nate rushed to Jason Johnson's front door, carrying the rubber chicken.

Chapter 18

Something Even More Terrifying Than Cooties

Nate and Ed were the last guests to arrive at the party.

Actually, Ed wasn't a guest. The invitation never said "Bring a rubber chicken."

The birthday party was fantastic. Just as Jason had promised, there was a huge cake with extra frosting, a dragon piñata filled with a ton of candy and real money, and six different video games going at all times with six pro gamers helping out.

There were also make-your-own sundaes with seven kinds of ice cream and thirty-eight toppings. Though Nate thought that bean sprouts, garlic, and diced pickles really shouldn't count as ice cream toppings.

Also, there were twelve different kinds of pizza, including Nate's favorite, the sausage-pepperoni-ham-meatball-bacon-steak combo.

None of the boys were mad at Nate anymore—except for Hulk Paine, but he didn't like anyone.

Nate ate so much pizza and ice cream that he barely had room for birthday cake.

As Nate was finishing his third slab of cake, Ed said, "This party is awful."

"Are you cuckoo?" Nate asked. "I'm having the best time of my life."

"Yeah, your friends are all here. I was hoping at least they'd include a few of my kind."

"Chickens?" Nate asked.

"Rubber chickens," Ed said.

Nate pointed to the appetizers on the kitchen counter. "At least they have deviled eggs and chicken fingers."

Ed grimaced. "Yuck."

"Hey, Nate," Jason said. "Are you talking to your rubber chicken doll again?"

"No! Of course not!" Nate said. "And Ed is not a doll."

"Ed? You named him?" Jason raised his eyebrows.

"He named himself," Nate said.

"My *mother* named me," Ed told Nate.

"Actually, Ed's rubber chicken mother

named him," Nate told Jason.

"He's a plastic toy!" Jason shouted. "Toys don't have mothers!"

"How dare he insult my mother!" Ed's beady eyes watered and his beak quivered.

Jason grabbed the rubber chicken. "Who wants to play catch?" he yelled.

A bunch of boys who had been outside burping "For He's a Jolly Good Fellow" screamed, "Yeah!" and "I do!" and "Me!" and . . . well, you get the point. They all wanted to play catch.

Jason tossed Ed toward his friends.

"Agh!" Ed said as he flew through the air. "I'm getting dizzy!"

Jason yelled, "Heads up! Here comes the rubber chicken doll!"

113

"I'm not a doll," Ed protested.

"Help!" Ed screamed as he landed in the backyard bushes. "I hope there aren't any snakes in here."

Nate rushed over and rescued him.

Then Nate screamed in terror. "I found something much worse than snakes! Something slimier and grosser!"

"What?" all the boys yelled.

"Girls!" Nate shouted, "Lisa and Ashley are hiding in the bushes!"

The girls stood up.

The boys screamed, **"Cooties! Bleck!"** and ran away.

"Boys are disgusting," Lisa said as she picked out leaves, dirt, and a family of beetles from her hair.

"This birthday party is a bore," Ashley said.

Nate pointed. "The front door's that way."

"But—" Lisa started to say.

Nate interrupted her. "I'll walk you out."

After Nate opened the front door for the girls, he discovered something even more terrifying than the sight of Lisa and Ashley in the bushes. He let out a bloodcurdling scream.

So did Ed.

So did everyone at the party, including the six pro gamers.

They all stared at the open doorway in horror.

Chapter 19
Told You So

Standing in Jason Johnson's doorway was

Mrs. Crabpit.

Nate and Lisa glanced around the

room. The other kids were cowering behind

couches, coffee tables, and chairs. The six pro gamers ran out the back door. Jason hid inside his sister's dollhouse.

"Why are you . . . ?" Nate started to say. "What are you . . . ? How did you . . . ? Who told you about the party?" he finally asked.

"You did, Natey." Mrs. Crabpit smiled at him.

Nate shuddered.

"It was on that note you wrote to me."

"But I crossed it out," Nate said.

"My vision's been super lately," Mrs. Crabpit explained. "I read it just fine."

She rushed over to the dollhouse, opened the door, and said hello to Jason.

Mrs. Crabpit's odor followed her. In fact, it not only followed her, it spread all over the room, through the house, and around most

117

of Arizona. Traces of her stink were even sniffed in California, Utah, New Mexico, and South Dakota.

Jason's mom called out from the kitchen, "What's that horrible smell?"

Jason plugged his nose and muttered, "I don't think my house will ever be the same again."

"I tried to tell you she was coming," Lisa muttered to her brother. "Ashley and I came over here to try to help."

"Um, gee, look at the time." Michael Perez stood up and stared at his wrist, though he wasn't wearing a watch. "I have to go water my plants now."

"Me too," Dan the Dawdler said.

"Yeah, what *he* said," Grant Sinker said.

"Ditto," most of the other boys said.

"Exactly," the rest of the boys said.

"Wait!" Lisa shouted. "Mrs. Crabpit, would you like to go to the mall with Ashley and me? If you stay here, you'll just have to listen to the boys' fake fart contests."

"The mall sounds like a lot more fun." Mrs. Crabpit rubbed her eyes. "Hmm, the last few days my eyesight seemed really great. Now it's faded back to how it used to be."

"I think there's an eye doctor at the mall," Lisa said. "You can have your vision checked there. Also, you can get some deodorant. I'll even pay for it."

Nate opened the front door and gave Mrs. Crabpit a little push. "Bye bye. Thanks for stopping by," he said.

"I'll be right out," Lisa told Mrs. Crabpit. Then she slammed the front door behind her. "I told you I could help you," she said to Nate.

"You were right. Thank you for all your help," Nate said.

"And I told you sometimes things don't seem to be working out, but they really do in the end," Ed said.

"Thank you, Ed, for *trying* to help," Nate said.

Lisa grabbed Ed. "Now if I have to go shopping with Mrs. Crabpit, then you do too."

"**Agh!**" Ed cried as Lisa headed for Mrs. Crabpit's stinky car. "This is working out well for everyone but me! I was better off in the trash can!"